CHRISTMAS
MANDALAS
COLORING BOOK

Marty Noble

Dover Publications, Inc.
Mineola, New York

This festive collection of Christmas coloring pages from artist Marty Noble combines familiar yuletide designs and motifs with the appealing circular pattern of the mandala. Perfect for getting into the holiday spirit, use your artistic imagination to add color to snowmen, mistletoe, Santa Claus, angels, elves, snowflakes, and other images of Christmas cheer.

Copyright

Copyright © 2014 by Dover Publications, Inc.
All rights reserved.

Bibliographical Note

Christmas Mandalas Coloring Book, first published by Dover Publications, Inc., in 2014, is a revised edition of the work originally published by Dover in 2013.

International Standard Book Number

ISBN-13: 978-0-486-79188-3
ISBN-10: 0-486-79188-2

Manufactured in the United States by RR Donnelley
79188206   2015
www.doverpublications.com

SEASON'S GREETINGS